Moose for Kids
(Moose Are Like That)

By Jeff Fair

NorthWord
PRESS, INC
Box 1360, Minocqua, WI 54548

DEDICATION

For all my Sister's children

— Jeff Fair

Photography Copyright ©1992 Michael H. Francis
Copyright ©1992
NorthWord Press, Inc.
P.O. Box 1360
Minocqua, WI 54548

ISBN 1-55971-187-6

Edited by Greg Linder
Designed by Russell S. Kuepper
All photos by Michael H. Francis except:
Robert W. Baldwin, pp. 6, 10, 28, 44
Illustrations by Sandy Stevens

For a free catalog describing NorthWord's line of books
and gift items, call toll free 1-800-336-5666.

Printed in Singapore.

Library of Congress Cataloging-in-Publication Data

Fair, Jeff
        Moose for kids : moose are like that / by Jeff Fair.
            p.   cm. -- (Wildlife for kids series : 7th)
        Summary : Describes the habitat, physical characteristics, and
behavior of the moose of the wild north country.
        ISBN 1-55971-187-6
        1. Moose--Juvenile literature. [1. Moose.]   I. Title.
    II. Series.
    QL737.U55F35 1992
    599.73'57--dc20
                                                        92-25080
                                                            CIP
                                                             AC

Forget about your chores for a while. And your spelling and your piano lessons and your video games and your cousin Arthur who is such an angel. It's time for some fresh air. Let's take a trip into the northwoods. We'll look for a moose's trail and maybe even find a moose at the end of it. Bring your wool shirt and a good pair of boots. It gets cold and muddy up here.

The great northwoods stretches from Maine and Labrador to Alaska.
Smell the evergreen air and the moldy aroma of muck from the marsh.
Around us, deep forests of spruce and fir hold silence and secrets.
You could get lost for a long time in this country, if you wanted to.
Wild things live here: loons and ravens and wolves. Bears belong to
these woods, and mink frogs live in the bogs. But moose symbolize
the wild north country best of all. This country is their home.

Moose make their meals from plants that grow here. They need the cool woods and open waters to survive summer's heat. This north-country landscape contains marshes and muskeg bogs, lakes and ponds, and meadows in the vast forest made when lightning has kindled a fire or loggers have cut down trees. The best moose foods grow in these meadows.

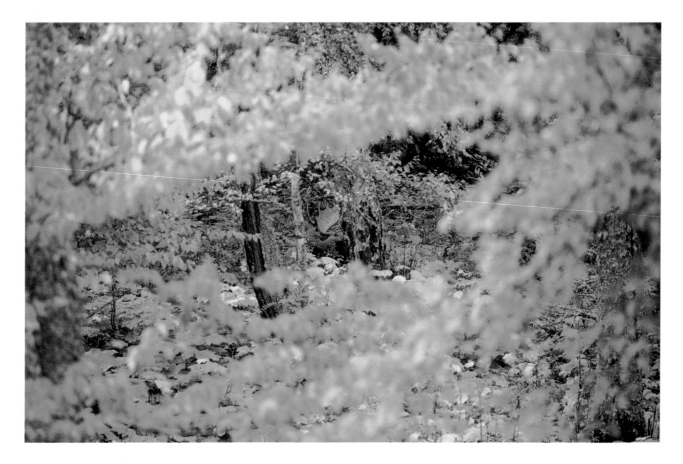

The native Algonquians, Indian people of the north country, gave the moose its name many years ago. Moose means "he who eats off trees and shrubs," or simply "twig eater." Algonquians believed that moose were good omens. If you dream of moose often, they said, you will live long.

The moose supplied the Algonquian people with many of the things they needed. Its hide became their clothing and shelter. From its bones and antlers, they fashioned tools. Its flesh—up to 700 pounds of muscle from a single moose—fed a native family all through the long northern winter.

You might say we still consider moose to be good omens, although most people today just say they feel lucky to see one. Moose provide some of us with food and mittens, and they give all of us something to marvel at. Mounted moose heads (with those glass eyes that follow you around) hang in places of honor in many north-country lodges. We wonder how such a large creature keeps itself secret and makes its living in the harsh wilderness of the northwoods.

7

You'd recognize a moose, wouldn't you? Watch for an animal as big as a horse, with four long, skinny legs. If it has a long head with a little beard (called a dewlap) at its throat, big ears like a mule, a drooping nose in front and a tiny tail hidden in back, then you've found a moose. And if you see a set of antlers attached in front of its ears, then it's a male, called a bull moose. A big rack of antlers is the crown of this king of the northwoods.

The awesome size of a moose makes your knees wobble when you see one. A big moose stands six feet tall at its shoulders and weighs more than 1,000 pounds. That's heavier than four refrigerators.

But you have to look hard to find one. Moose are brown, usually dark brown, the same color as marsh mud and forest shadows. And despite their huge size, moose move through the woods as quietly as shadows. Moose prefer to travel alone and stick to the wilder country. They usually appear when you don't expect them to. Moose are like that.

To really look for a moose, keep a sharp eye out for antlers, ripples on the pond, and big old tree stumps that walk. Watch for the signs it leaves behind. Moose make a lot of footprints in snow and soft ground. These hoof tracks help us find moose, or at least know where they've been. A moose track looks like a heart, or like a pair of teardrops about six inches long. The sharper end of each track points in the direction that the moose traveled.

In winter, moose leave behind piles of round or oval pellets bigger than large grapes. These pellets are really just packed sawdust, and they don't smell like anything you couldn't bring home.

In the summer, moose droppings may be softer because moose eat softer, fresher plants at this time of year. They look like what you might find behind a happy Hereford cow. Call them moose pies. On a sunny hillside, you may notice a faint barnyard perfume. But there are no cattle in these woods. It's moose sign that you smell. Follow your nose. And watch where you step—you might learn something.

Now look over here. See the big patch of grass matted down in the meadow? Why, it's the size of your mattress at home. But this is a moose bed instead. If we had been quieter, we might have caught the moose snoozing.

In the muddy north-country spring, when cackling geese return on the warm wind and loons come back to dance, moose leave the drier forests and slip into the moist muskegs and thickets of young aspen. After the long, hungry winter, moose begin to fatten up again on a diet of fresh new leaves and stems of willow, aspen, and maple.

Moose won't reach very far for their food. They browse on leaves and twigs between four and ten feet above the ground—easy pickings for the long-legged moose. You won't catch a moose grazing on grass very often. Grass is a long way down from a moose mouth. With such long front legs and such a short neck, a moose has to kneel to touch the ground with its muzzle.

A moose has front teeth on the bottom, but not on top. It partly cuts and partly tears off each bite of browse. To reach higher twigs, a moose sometimes walks right up to a small tree, straddles it between his front legs, and keeps walking, bending the tree over. When he reaches the top of the tree, he eats his fill. When he walks away, the tree springs back up. It looks as though the moose had to be twelve feet tall to reach up there. This is as close as a moose will come to playing a trick on you.

Moose eat the smooth bark of aspen and maple trees, too. They scrape the bark right off the tree and into their mouths with the two front teeth on their lower jaw. Afterward, the tree looks as though someone scraped its trunk with two sharp spoons, side by side. You may be close to a moose if you find white, moist wood beneath these scraped places. Check for tracks. Stand very still. Is a moose watching you? Maybe. Moose are like that.

You may not find the moose, but you can be pretty sure that it will return next year in the same season. Moose rove around for different foods at different times of year, but they don't go more than a few miles away. If no one puts up a shopping center or plunks down a highway where you find your moose sign, the moose will probably be back next year.

In May and June you won't see many cow moose. Most of them are pregnant now. Pregnant cows find secret places near lakeshores and on small islands. Here they give birth to their calves, usually single ones, but sometimes twins. The reddish-brown moose calves weigh only 25 to 35 pounds, and they arrive with four long, wobbly legs that are hard to control at first. A cow licks its calf a lot, and the two stick close together. By its third or fourth day, a moose calf could outrun you, but before that it would make an easy meal for a bear or a pack of wolves if its mother weren't there to protect it.

A defensive cow moose lays back her ears, lowers her head, and runs
between her calf and whatever threatens it. Long hairs on the back of
her neck and shoulders stand up like a dark mane. The threat might
be a bear poking around in the pasture. Or it might be a pack of wolves
challenging her from several sides. Or the threat might even be you, if
you surprise the cow moose. The cow can kick high and hard up front
and like a mule in back. An angry moose is a tough critter to argue
with. Many bears and wolves decide to go elsewhere and look for an
easier meal.

Moose look pretty scruffy in late spring. Big patches of last year's hair peel off to make way for a dark new coat. You might find a patch of moose hair hanging in alder branches or floating at the water's edge. The long, hollow guard hairs feel like the bristles of a brush and twist like rope between your fingers. By next winter, the new guard hairs will be up to eight or ten inches long. Between them, underneath, the moose will grow a warm, wooly undercoat.

Calves follow the cows out of hiding as soon as they have their legs under control. By tagging along closely, they learn to swim and to chew on the right plants. Moose calves don't stay little for long. First they grow taller, then they grow longer. Their bones will grow for seven years, but they grow fastest during that first summer. By autumn, when they stop nursing, moose calves weigh 400 pounds.

Wildlife of another kind thrives in the northwoods during the warm season. On quiet evenings you hear them by the millions, revving their little engines. Black flies, deer flies, moose flies, and mosquitoes torment anything with blood. You'll want to bring plenty of bug repellent, even though it never really works, and maybe some mosquito netting to cover your head. Moose bat at bugs with their big ears or go swimming to be left in peace. Mostly, moose just put up with bugs. Moose are like that.

21

Summer is a good time to see a moose or two in the water. A cow and her calf, maybe. Or a couple of young bulls who have learned to put up with each other. They cool off in the water and eat the juicy pond weeds.

Look for moose in the early morning and at dusk, especially after storms and when the wind dies down. On a quiet day you might hear one over in the bay, mucking around on those saucer-sized hooves and bobbing for lilies. A huge head goes under the water. A long time passes. Then the head rises and water streams off the antlers and gushes out of a half-open mouth filled with greens. The head shakes, sending arcs of spray across the pond. Silver droplets tinkle onto the water's surface as a long jaw chews, moving sideways. The humming of flies returns.

A moose will dive down 18 feet for a good bite of pond weed and float up tail-first while it's munching. Valves in its nostrils keep the water out of its nose. A moose swims with its entire head above water. It can swim for miles, and almost as fast as two people can paddle a canoe.

A moose can move even faster in water that would sink you to your ears. That's only belly-high to a moose. With her long legs pumping like pistons under her large, dark body, a cow moose hurrying to protect her calf in shallow water looks like a living locomotive. Those stilt-like legs work the same way in three or four feet of mud or snow. Moose rarely panic, even if they get stuck. They just rest, bat their ears at the flies (or snowflakes), and then lumber on. Moose are like that.

A moose in a hurry usually trots. Moose can gallop up to 35 miles per hour, faster than cars go on city streets, but they rarely do. They don't often jump, either. With those long legs they can step over almost anything that's too wide to go around.

SMACK!
What was that?
A moose? No.
Look there on
the pond. It
was a beaver,
slapping its
tail. Like
moose, beavers
eat bark and
aspen and
maple twigs.
They cut down
and carry off
the same trees

that moose munch on. But beavers help moose, too. They make ponds where moose can eat and cool off. And after the beavers leave, their ponds drain away to become dry meadows where young aspens and birches and maples grow. It's a pretty good deal for a moose.

An adult moose packs up to 50 pounds of leaves, twigs, stems, and bark each day into the four stomachs it carries around inside its big belly. Like cattle,

goats, deer, and other animals, called ruminants, moose depend on this four-part system to help them digest their vegetables.

In summer, moose continue to eat leaves and twigs as well as pond weeds. Sometimes they just want leaves. A moose will bite across a willow branch and slide his head toward the tip of the branch, stripping off the leaves in his mouth. After some chewing, but not much, he'll swallow this mouthful into his first stomach and strip off more leaves. Later he'll burp the leaves up for more chewing and swallow them to the second stomach, where he begins digesting them.

A moose may allow a girl or boy of average curiosity and adventurous spirit to walk up fairly close in the summertime. Sometimes too close. Don't get any ideas about rubbing that velvety soft muzzle. It isn't easy to alarm a moose, but if you get too close, the whole valley will hear about it. Moose are like that.

And don't think for a moment that the moose doesn't know you're nearby. Her eyes work independently, so she only needs one to keep an eye on you. See how her ears are pointed your way? She heard your lightest footsteps in the grass. And since most of the inside of her long face is nose, she noticed your scent a long time ago. You may not smell like a hungry bear, but you probably don't smell any better than one. To a moose, that is.

A bull moose grows his antlers all summer. A very young bull grows only spikes, but a big bull's rack of antlers may reach more than six feet across and weigh over 75 pounds. Growing antlers are covered by a soft, fuzzy skin called velvet. The velvet carries blood to the antlers, and the blood deposits calcium that makes bone. That's what an antler is—bone.

By September the antlers have finished growing, and the velvet dries and itches. Bulls rub it off against trees and thrash their racks in the bushes. You can see where a moose rubbed his rack. Other moose see this, too, and know there's a bull in the neighborhood.

Polished antlers shine like mirrors when they get wet. Watch the distant shore on sunny days for bright flashes. It could be a bull moose, or it could be the glint of sun off the canoe paddle of someone who has a good moose story to tell.

When my friend Phil came up to the north country one autumn, he wanted to see a moose. I told him I could find him one. So I took him over to our cabin on the river. We hiked up the ridge and saw tooth marks on the maples. We sneaked into the swamp and saw moose droppings. We crossed the clearing and found tracks and aspen sprouts with their tops browsed off. But we didn't find a moose. Phil said I wasn't much of a moose guide. I told him moose can be hard to find. "Moose are like that," I said.

Before supper I paddled the canoe up the river to catch some trout. After the sun went down and the air turned cold, a thick mist rose over the water. I heard a strange noise as I floated back down the river. It came out of the dark fog near our cabin. It sounded like a cross between a rusty car door hinge and a fog horn—deep, but with a squeak in it. Something like *HRRONK!* or *REEUMK!* I just knew it was Phil, hiding in the bushes and trying to grunt like a moose. (Phil is like that.) I made plans to sneak up and scare him.

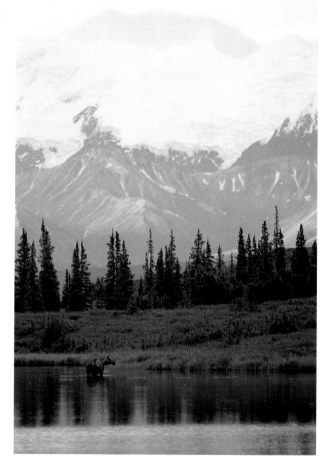

But when I rounded the bend, I found a big bull moose instead of Phil. The moose stood in four feet of water, but I still had to look up at him from the canoe. He took a step or two, splashed his broad antlers in the river (first one side, then the other), then raised his dripping muzzle and bellowed. *HRRONK!* It was the beginning of the rut, or breeding season, and he was calling to other moose. I floated quietly past him and found Phil back at the cabin.

"Were you making that noise?" he asked me.

"Phil," I told him, "you missed your moose."

During the rut, prime bulls with big racks and years of experience pick fights with each other. You don't want a moose to get the wrong idea about you at this time of year. Bad-tempered bulls have chased many a trespasser up a tree. Watch from a distance. And if you ever meet a big bull face to face in the fall, remember this piece of advice: Don't mess with a moose.

A rutting bull stares at his challenger and circles him with stiff, confident steps. (Young bulls get nowhere when they try this. They just have to wait and grow.) Tension builds, moose heads lower, and antlers bang together like trees falling into each other. Usually one bull wins the fight before hurting the other one badly.

The cow stands quietly nearby in a place she has selected. She awaits the attention of the winner. The bull was fighting so he could be with her. After the rut, in November and December, the big bulls drop their antlers. Smaller bulls who didn't use theirs as much carry them as late as March. Dropped antlers disappear quickly, gnawed by mice and squirrels that recycle the calcium into their own bones.

Now it's winter. There's a moaning in the air. Wolves howling? No, not this time. Just the arctic wind. At 40 below zero, frost stings right through your warmest moosehide mittens and your heaviest boots. Your breath would freeze right to your beard, if you had one. Ice covers the ponds, and snow buries the bushes. Lush summer foods are gone now. Moose have moved to drier forests, where they browse on tough, leafless winter twigs that are less nourishing and harder to digest.

When the snow reaches belly-high, moose take shelter in stands of fir and hemlock. They may gather in groups now and stay sheltered in this winter cover for days. They browse on fir boughs or nearby willows and nap in the snow in their thick winter coats. Where food is scarce and winters are hard, moose eat all the fir boughs they can reach. In this winter range you'll see a browse line where no green twig is left below ten feet off the ground.

Most moose survive the long north-country winters, but they pay a price. By the time spring melts the frost and brings new plant growth (moose food!), a moose has lost one-third of its body weight. Imagine losing one-third of your weight. You'd look skinnier. So does a moose in May.

Last year's calf, a year old, gets the surprise of its life this spring. Its mother suddenly nips and kicks at it, sending it away. She prefers to give birth again in private. The yearling may rejoin its mother later in the year, or it might wander off. Yearlings are the most adventuresome moose when it comes to discovering new places to live.

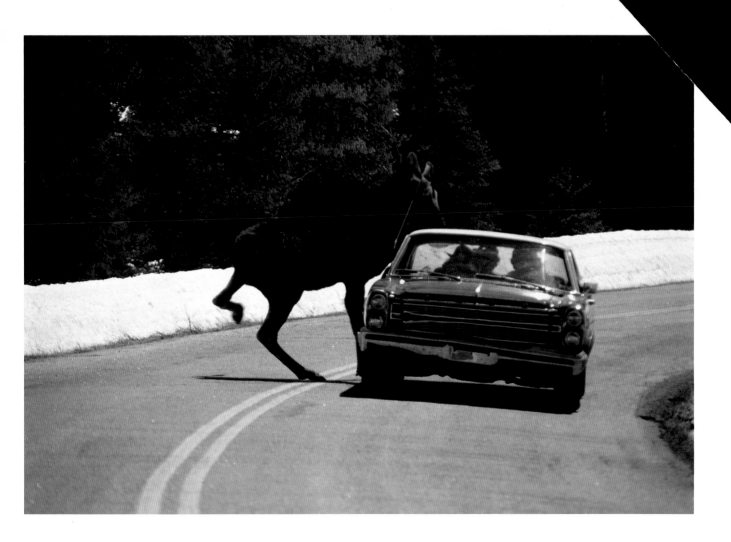

In spring and summer, many people watch for moose near highways.
Moose like to lick the salt that is spread on roads through the winter.
Some moose, especially those adventuresome yearlings, wander across
roads where drivers don't expect them. A driver can't always see a
dark moose at night. This isn't good for the moose. It isn't good for
drivers, either.

t one million moose live in North America today. One hundred
ago, fewer moose lived on this continent, mostly because people
illed too many. Today hunters continue to hunt moose (but not too
many). Bears and wolves eat moose calves. Yet moose are returning to
their former homes along the southern border of their range, where
more people live. Here, believe it or not, deer carry the greatest threat
to moose.

Deer live across the continent
and north to the southern edge
of moose range. A little parasite
called the brain worm infects
both deer and moose. When a
deer has this disease, it stays
healthy. You'd never even know
it had brain worm. But when
the brain worm infects a moose,
it causes damage. The infected
moose loses control, walks
blindly into things, becomes
paralyzed, and finally dies. A
moose living around deer can be
infected by the parasite at any
time. The brain worm—and the
heat, too—keep moose from
expanding their range
southward out of the
northwoods.

Where I live, in New Hampshire, moose are coming back after being gone for many years. If you lived here, you might get a visit from one of those adventurous yearlings one May morning. Imagine a wild moose looking into the window of your cabin. But don't expect it to stay very long. What if it saw another moose's head sticking out of the wall over the fireplace? Or, even scarier yet, what if it saw a gangly

little creature in a wool shirt and boots, looking back through the window with a mouthful of corn flakes?

What would a moose do then? Well, probably just trot over to the edge of the woods and look back at you with at least one eye. Maybe with both. Then it would march right down to the bug-filled marsh for a bite of aspen, as though nothing unusual had happened. As though it never even saw you.

Moose are like that.

What To Call A Moose

One day a long time ago, up in moose country, my friend Scott asked me if I had ever heard his moose call. I told him I'd seen a moose fly (the insect, I meant), but I had never heard a moose call. He said he'd do it for me. So he cupped his hands and shouted, as loudly as he could, "HEEEEEERE MOOOOOOOOOOOOOOSE." Scott studies birds, and he thought this was funny.

Some people, hunters mostly, really do call moose. They roll a large piece of birch bark into a horn and try to sound like a cow moose that's looking for company. This works sometimes, but you ought to know what you're saying to the moose before you try it.

Moose, elk, deer, and caribou all belong to the deer family. If you hear someone say that moose are our biggest deer, they mean that moose are the biggest members of the deer family. That's a fact.

Scientists call the moose by its Latin name, *Alces alces*. (Say it like this: *Al sees, Al sees*.) *Alces* means elk, which is OK because over in Europe they have moose but they call them elk. It's an old habit.

A new moose is called a *calf*, as you already know. When a calf turns one year old, it becomes a *yearling*. After that, it all depends. A female moose we call a *cow*. A cow is ready to be a mother when she is four years old.

A male moose we call a *bull*. By the time he's two years old, a bull feels ready to be a father, but the older bulls usually disagree. We call this young male a *teen bull* until he can challenge the big guys and really be a father. Then we'll call him a *prime bull*. A bull stays in his prime through the ages of six to ten or twelve. After that we call him a *senior bull*.

Moose may live to be 20 years old or more. You can call an old moose tired, but not retired. For as long as it lives, a moose must continue to make its living. No moose retires until it lies down one day in its final bed and donates its body to the flies and coyotes, and its antlers to the mice.

All wild creatures are like that.